Learn About Rural Life

Life in a Forestry Community

Lizann Flatt

Crabtree Publishing Company
www.crabtreebooks.com

Author: Lizann Flatt
Editor-in-Chief: Lionel Bender
Editors: Simon Adams and Molly Aloian
Proofreader: Crystal Sikkens
Editorial director: Kathy Middleton
Photo research: Lizann Flatt and Ben White
Designer: Ben White
Production coordinator: Katherine Berti
Production: Kim Richardson
Prepress technician: Margaret Amy Salter
Consultant: Heather L. Montgomery, DragonFly
  Environmental Education Programs

Front cover (main image): Workers load logs into
  a logging truck in British Columbia, Canada.
Back cover: A woodworker prepares a piece of lumber.
Title page: A loaded logging truck in a forest in
  British Columbia, Canada

Photographs and reproductions
Alamy: Chris Cheadle: front cover (main image)
District of Mackenzie: B. Coldwell: p. 22, 23, 25, 26, 27;
  C. Jackson: p. 12, 13, 14, 15, 16, 17, 18, 19
Getty Images: Uyen Le: p. 5; Lester Lefkowitz: p. 21;
  National Geographic: p. 24, 28; Bob Pool: p. 20
Istockphoto: back cover, page corner graphic, p. 1, 4, 6, 7,
  8, 9, 11, 29
Shutterstock: front cover (inset)
Topfoto: The Granger Collection: p. 10

Acknowledgments
Special thanks to:
Kerri Borne, Tourism Marketing Coordinator, District of
Mackenzie, and Alice Winkel, resident of Mackenzie, for
checking information and providing images for the book.

This book was produced for Crabtree Publishing
Company by Bender Richardson White.

Library and Archives Canada Cataloguing in Publication

Flatt, Lizann
    Life in a forestry community / Lizann Flatt.

(Learn about rural life)
Includes index.
ISBN 978-0-7787-5073-4 (bound).--ISBN 978-0-7787-5086-4 (pbk.)

    1. Forests and forestry--Juvenile literature. 2. Forestry and
community--Juvenile literature. 3. Mackenzie (B.C.)--Juvenile
literature. I. Title. II. Series: Learn about rural life

SD376.F53 2009   j634.9   C2009-903850-1

Library of Congress Cataloging-in-Publication Data

Flatt, Lizann.
    Life in a forestry community / Lizann Flatt.
       p. cm. -- (Learn about rural life)
    Includes index.
    ISBN 978-0-7787-5086-4 (pbk. : alk. paper) -- ISBN 978-0-7787-
5073-4 (reinforced library binding : alk. paper)
    1. Forests and forestry--British Columbia--Juvenile literature. 2.
Forestry and community--British Columbia--Juvenile literature. 3.
Mackenzie (B.C.)--Juvenile literature. I. Title. II. Series: Learn
about rural life.

SD146.B8F53 2010
634.909711'82--dc22

                                                      2009024552

4695

Crabtree Publishing Company
www.crabtreebooks.com   1-800-387-7650

**Published
in Canada
Crabtree Publishing**
616 Welland Ave.
St. Catharines, Ontario
L2M 5V6

**Published in
the United States
Crabtree Publishing**
PMB16A
350 Fifth Ave., Suite 3308
New York, NY 10118

**Published in the
United Kingdom
Crabtree Publishing**
White Cross Mills
High Town, Lancaster
LA1 4XS

**Published
in Australia
Crabtree Publishing**
386 Mt. Alexander Rd.
Ascot Vale (Melbourne)
VIC 3032

Contents

Where People Live

There are about 6.8 billion people in the world. Most people live in houses or apartments. When thousands of homes are built alongside stores, offices, **factories**, and hotels, they form big **towns** or **cities**. These are known as **urban areas**. When houses are built in the countryside in small groups, they form **villages** and small towns. These are **rural areas**.

▼ A large city such as New York City in the United States, is an urban area. More than 8,000,000 people live here. It is filled with busy, noisy streets, traffic, and buildings.

Banff in Alberta, Canada, is a rural place. About 6,700 people live in the town. It is built among forests and mountains.

Wherever people live, they need food, fresh water, and materials to build their homes. They also need **fuel** for cooking and to heat and light their homes. In rural places, people live, work, and play close together. Everyone soon gets to know everyone else. The people form a **community**. In urban areas, there may be several separate communities. This book looks at everyday life in Mackenzie, British Columbia, Canada, a rural community that depends mostly on forestry.

What is Forestry?

Forestry is caring for land that is filled with trees. People who look after forests are called foresters. They **harvest**, or cut down, trees in a forest. They also plant new trees to make sure there will be a steady supply for years to come. Foresters also make sure the forests are healthy. Trees stop soil from being washed away and provide homes and food for forest animals. Trees also help rivers stay clean.

▼ Foresters use logging machines and trucks to cut down and remove **coniferous** trees. They are used for softwood lumber.

Once trees are cut down and the branches are removed, they are called logs. Cutting down trees is called **logging**. When logs are cut into usable pieces, the wood is called **lumber**. There are two main types of lumber based on the type of tree from which it came. Softwood lumber comes from coniferous trees. Hardwood lumber comes from **deciduous** trees.

From the Forests

Wood from forests is used in many ways. Logs are used to make cabins. Boards or lumber are used to build houses and barns. Thin sheets of lumber called veneers can be glued together to make plywood for furniture. Even the tiniest pieces called wood **fibers** and **sawdust** are used to make paper and cardboard.

▼ A carpenter uses lumber to build a wood frame for a house. The lumber has been cut down to standard sizes at a factory called a **sawmill**.

▲ Paper is made out of tiny pieces of wood that are specially treated at a factory called a **paper mill**.

Every day, people use or see things made from wood. Doors, furniture, pencils, telephone poles, boxes, books, tissues, and popsicle sticks are all made of wood. Maple syrup, a fabric called rayon, and some plastics, glues, inks, and varnishes are all made from trees. Many people in the world burn wood as a fuel for cooking and to heat their homes.

Forestry in North America

Native North Americans have been using trees for thousands of years. The first **settlers** started logging in the 1600s. They took trees from the forests of Maine and Virginia. Later, in the 1800s, logging became a big **industry** in parts of Ontario and Quebec in Canada, and in Michigan and Pennsylvania in the United States. Today, the main logging areas are in Alaska, Washington, and British Columbia.

▼ These horses are pulling a sled of logs out of a forest in about 1895. Horses were used as work animals before trucks were invented.

Many forests, such as this one in Oregon, are now national parks. In these areas, little or no logging is allowed.

At first, settlers cut down trees to clear land for farms, roads, and houses. At the same time, loggers would cut down trees and sell the logs and lumber for money. It seemed like the huge forests would last forever. People didn't realize they were harming the water, soil, and wildlife in the forests. Around 1900, the U.S. and Canadian governments each started their own **Forestry Service** to look after and protect large forests.

Welcome to Mackenzie

Mackenzie is a small town in the province of British Columbia on Canada's west coast. It is a rural area surrounded by forests. The nearest cities are a two-hour car ride away. In 1793, explorer Sir Alexander Mackenzie camped here, and the town is named after him. In winter, the temperature is usually below 14°F (–10°C). In summer, it can reach 95°F (35°C).

▼ A sign welcomes visitors as they enter Mackenzie on the main two-lane highway into town.

▲ A view of Mackenzie as seen from the air. The town is small enough to walk everywhere.

In the 1960s, the Canadian government built a **dam** on a nearby river to make electricity. Some of the forest was cut down to clear the land. Sawmills were set up to **process** the logs. In 1975, a forestry company finished building roads, houses, schools, stores, a water supply, and a hospital. Families who worked in the local forestry industry moved in. As a result, Mackenzie grew.

Life in the Town

Mackenzie has a lot of things for people to do. A recreation center contains a pool, curling rink, arena, and library. In summer, there are two lakes for swimming, boating, and fishing. Children attend one of the two elementary schools or the high school. When they are not at school, children like to cross-country ski, skate, mountain bike, and play lacrosse, hockey, and basketball.

▼ The library has books and DVDs for people to borrow and computers for them to use. It also provides information about events in the town.

Most houses in the town are low-rise buildings. They have a wood frame built with lumber from the forest.

The elementary schools have almost 200 students each, and the high school has nearly 300 students. The town has a small shopping mall, but no movie theater. Children rent movies, or the school sometimes holds a movie night. In summer, it is possible to see a moose, a coyote, a black bear, or a grizzly bear wandering in the town. The animals come from the forest.

Celebrating the Seasons

Mackenzie is surrounded by the natural world so people celebrate the seasons. In June, the town holds Sir Alexander Mackenzie Days to honor its **founder**. Events include a community barbecue, a triathlon—a running, swimming, and cycling race—Kids' Fest, and a toy duck race. At other times, people take boats on the lakes and compete to catch the biggest fish.

▼ In spring, people visit local garden centers and plant nurseries where they can buy young plants for their gardens.

On Sir Alexander Mackenzie Days, the town puts on a street parade. Sport, youth, and social groups make their own floats and join the parade.

In the winter, the lakes freeze over and the area gets about 11 feet (3.5 meters) of snow. Then Mackenzie holds its Winter Carnival. Food-tasting, ice fishing, and games are just some of the many activities. There is even a polar bear swim, but people just pretend to be like polar bears. Really, they swim in the pool.

A Forestry Family

Most families in Mackenzie live within the town, not in the countryside. Adults that work in a forestry mill or office go to work and come home daily. Those that are loggers, who harvest the trees, often work away from home for three to four weeks at a time. They live in a logging camp close to the forest. Then they get one week off to spend at home.

▼ Loggers use large cranes, loaders, and trucks to move the huge logs from the forest to sawmills and paper mills.

When parents are not working, they often take their children to a lake. There they play on the shore or in the water, rest, or have a meal by a campfire.

The winter shutdown is from the beginning of October to the end of November. This is when **maintenance** work is done on the equipment. Work in the forest stops again from about March to May while the snow and frost melt. The water from melting snow makes the roads too muddy and soft for the lumber vehicles to travel on. In the summer, if it gets too dry, work in the forest stops again because sparks from machinery can start a fire.

In the Forest

Foresters decide which trees will be cut. Loggers do the cutting. Using a chainsaw, a logger first makes a wedge-shaped cut on the tree trunk close to the ground. This is called an undercut. The logger then saws through the rest of the trunk. The tree falls toward the side with the undercut. This is how loggers know where a tree will fall which makes logging safer.

▼ This logger, or lumberjack, has made the first cut with his chainsaw. Once the tree is down, the logger will cut it into shorter lengths and cut off the branches.

Logs are loaded onto logging trucks by cranes or grabbers. Most logs are taken out of the forest this way.

Large machines are used to do some of the work. Tree shears work like a huge pair of scissors, cutting down trees quickly. A machine called a tree harvester can do all the work of cutting down, removing branches, and cutting up trees. The logs are gathered in one area called a landing. They are then taken out of the forest. Many logs are carried by truck, but some are tied into rafts and pulled on water. Others are loaded onto barges or rail cars.

At the Mills

Factories called mills make logs into other things. A sawmill makes lumber. First the **bark** is taken off the logs. Then each log is sawed into pieces until it is a pile of boards. The boards are trimmed by smaller saws and then graded, or separated into groups. Hardwood and softwood lumber are graded based on look, size, the type of wood, and what the wood is used for.

▼ Boards are long, thin strips of wood. Mill workers wear protective hats as moving loads can be very dangerous.

Once boards of lumber are graded, they are left to dry or are put in warm-air ovens to get rid of moisture, or dampness, in the wood. Then their surfaces are made smooth using machines called planers. All this processing makes small pieces of wood and sawdust. These are usually sent to special mills to make paper, cards, and cardboard. All this can take weeks.

Looking After the Forest

Foresters decide what jobs need to be done to keep the forest healthy. They decide which older trees are ready to be harvested. They plant new trees to make sure the forest continues to survive. They also study and learn about new types of trees that will grow quickly and resist diseases and insect pests.

▼ Where trees once stood, foresters turn over the soil and plant seedlings so new trees will grow. Sometimes they bring in young trees from elsewhere and plant these straight into the soil.

Firefighters from Mackenzie are always on-call to put out any forest fires that can spread to the town.

Pictures from space satellites give the foresters information about the forest. Areas where trees have disease show up in different colors. These trees can then be treated or removed to stop the disease from spreading. Forest fires help return **nutrients** to the soil and clear areas for new trees to grow. These fires are allowed to burn if they are no danger to people or buildings. Dangerous fires must be put out as quickly as possible.

Changing Lifestyle

Sales of wood products made in North America have fallen more and more. This has caused many mills in Mackenzie to shut down or lay off workers. Like many other forestry towns, Mackenzie is looking for ways to create new jobs for its **residents**. Metals, such as zinc, lead, silver, and gold, have been found near Mackenzie. **Mining** for these may offer jobs to people leaving forestry.

▼ Many people that used to work machinery in mills have learned to use computers. They can now help to run mines and new factories.

Towns are also trying to attract tourists.
Tourism creates jobs for people in
stores, hotels, restaurants, and at
local attractions. In Mackenzie during
the winter, there are mountains for
downhill skiing, and snowmobiling or
cross-country skiing trails to explore.
In warmer weather, activities such as
canoeing, kayaking, fishing, biking, and
camping let visitors enjoy the beauty
of the forests and lakes. Mackenzie's
rural location will help it to survive.

Forestry Around the World

North America produces much of the world's wood products. It uses many of these itself. The rest are sold to other countries. Forest products that are bought and sold throughout the world include logs or posts, lumber, panels, pulp and paper, and wood for fuel. India, China, Brazil, and Ethiopia make most of the world's wood fuel.

▼ Much of the forests of Brazil have been cut down to make room for raising cattle. This has often damaged the land and killed much wildlife.

Countries that have large areas of forest include Russia, China, Brazil, Sweden, and Finland. Forested regions all over the world are made up of different types of trees. Trees take in **carbon dioxide** and release **oxygen** that people need to breathe. They make Earth a place where people can live. People must look after forests and use them wisely.

Facts and Figures

World forests
More than 300 million people around the world live in forests. Nearly 4 billion hectares of forest cover Earth's surface, roughly 30 percent of its total land area.

How old is a tree?
You can count the growth rings of a tree stump to tell how old a tree was. A Bristlecone Pine tree in the White Mountains of California is believed to be 4,700 years old.

Paper Facts
Paper is made from fibers—long thin pieces of plant material. Most paper in North America is made from wood fiber, but it can also be made from cloth and other plant materials.

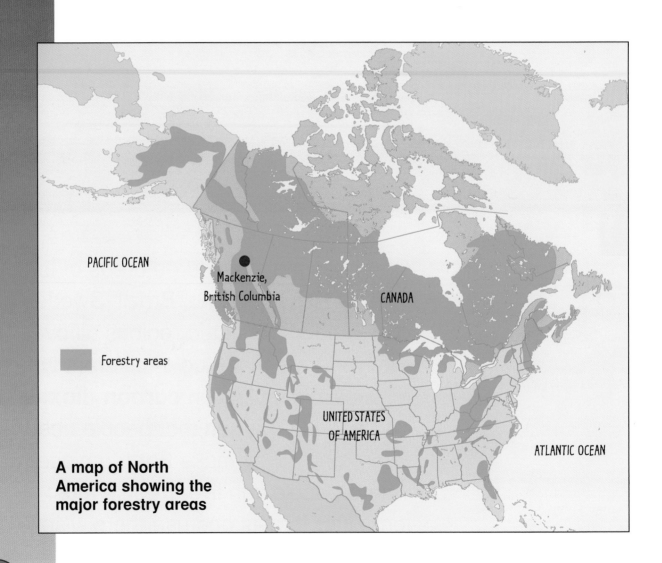

PACIFIC OCEAN

Mackenzie, British Columbia

CANADA

Forestry areas

UNITED STATES OF AMERICA

ATLANTIC OCEAN

A map of North America showing the major forestry areas

Glossary

bark The tough, outer layer of a tree trunk

carbon dioxide A gas in the air that trees take in and which people breathe out

city The largest urban area, with thousands of people, houses, offices, roads, and factories

community A group of people who live, work, and play close together

coniferous A type of tree that has cones to hold its seeds

dam A wall built across a river to hold back water

deciduous A type of tree that loses all its leaves in winter

factory A building where a lot of people work and make things

fiber Thin threads found in wood

Forestry Service A government department that looks after forests

founder A person who started something

fuel Something that produces energy to heat, light, or work a machine

harvest To cut down and collect plants or plant products

industry Workers, factories, mines, and equipment related to a resource such as coal, forestry, cars, and ships

logging Cutting down trees, done by a logger or lumberjack

lumber Usuable pieces of wood cut from logs

maintenance Checking and repairing to make sure something works

mining Removing useful materials from rock

nutrients Things in food that plants and animals need to stay healthy

oxygen A gas in the air that trees make which people need to breathe

paper mill A factory where paper is made

process To prepare, make ready, or change into something useful

residents The people who live in an area

rural area A small living area in the countryside

sawdust Very small pieces of wood made when sawing lumber

sawmill A place where lumber is cut up and made ready to use

settlers People who move into an area and set up homes

town A place where people live that has many houses, stores, offices, and factories. Small towns are rural, large towns are urban

urban area A built-up area such as a city or a large town

village A small rural area with a few houses

Further Information

Further Reading

Bishop, Nic. *Forest Explorer: A Lifesize Field Guide.* Scholastic Inc, 2004.

Drake, Jane and Love, Ann. *Cool Woods: A Trip Around the World's Boreal Forest.* Tundra, 2003.

Vogt, Richard C. *Rain Forests.* Simon & Schuster Children's Publishing, 2009.

Walsh, Ann and Cook Waldron, Kathleen. *Forestry A–Z.* Orca Book Publishing, 2008.

Web Sites

Forest Sites

www.naturalinquirer.org

www.smokeybear.com/kids/default.asp

Mackenzie and its History

www.settlerseffects.ca

www.district.mackenzie.bc.ca

Forest Conservation

www.theexplorationplace.com/eforest/

Index

Printed in the U.S.A.—CG